This book is for

.......Simon..................

As a gift from

......Raha....................

On

....

If you hadn't received this book as a gift, your friends haven't read it yet!

DR. RAHA ERNEST

BORN FREE
to
LIVE FREE

Unless otherwise indicated, all scripture quotations are taken from New King James Version (NKJV) of the Bible.

Scripture taken from the New King James Version®. Copyright © 1982 by Thomas Nelson. Used by permission. All rights reserved.

Wherever a testimony is used, conversations and names have been altered for privacy and to make the point clearer.

Born Free to Live Free
Born free to Grow free and Live free
by Raha Ernest

Cover Photo by Susana Coutinho on Unsplash
Cover design by Raha Ernest

Copyright © 2019 Raha Ernest

All rights reserved under international Copyright Law. No part of this book may be reproduced or transmitted in any form or by any means, electronic or mechanical, including photocopying, recording, or by any information storage and retrieval system, without the written permission of the publisher.

Thank you

Thank you for reading my book. Please review this book on <u>Amazon</u> to receive a free copy of my next book on kindle. While on Amazon, scroll down to find a tab with the title 'Write a customer review'. I need your feedback to make the next version better.

gratitudes

Thanks to friends who have proofread and encouraged me along the way. Thanks to Richard & Ali Guy, Tom Ogrodzinski, Lucy Curtis-Prior, Rev. Roger Williams, Donna-Rose Carter, Fern Watson, Bryn Richards, my wife Susan and many others. Your support is invaluable.

Mostly grateful to Andrew Wommack Ministries, my mother Mrs. Nsarye E. Urassa, and my late father Professor Ernest J.N Urassa

Table of Contents

Introduction	8
SEED	10
WOMB	24
INFANT	46
TODDLER	54
CHILD	64
TEEN	82
ADULT	100
FAMILY	122
Salvation	142
The Holy Spirit	144
Healing	146

INTRODUCTION

From the moment I accepted Jesus as my Lord and Saviour, a seed was planted in my heart. From that point forward, I started to grow with great awareness of my destiny. My heart provides a place for me to outgrow my spiritual childhood.

Firstly, I transformed into a *toddler*. Spiritual toddlers are those who are taking some *steps* to overcome the barriers that comes with being a baby Christian. They are those who have realised that crawling wouldn't get them through life. They are getting on their feet to take steps which will enable them to have real freedom.

Toddlers do eventually become spiritual teens. Teenagers would normally try to redefine their boundaries. As a spiritual teenager, I wanted to experience a life that was beyond my childhood boundaries. Like any teenager, I wanted to have a taste of a life with no limits.

That is my transformation as a Christian or Disciple. Like you, I am not born again to go to heaven. I am born again to grow again. We all have an opportunity to experience freedom beyond our spiritual birth and become more and more like Jesus.

1

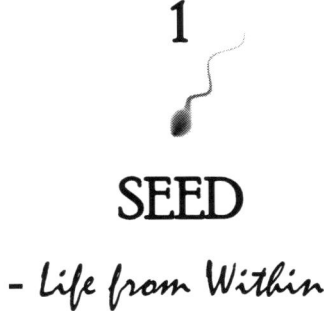

SEED

- Life from Within -

For something to be called a seed, it's future must be guaranteed. As such, even when the future of the world appears to be unpredictable, the future of a seed is fixed and cannot be changed. Every seed contains within itself the ability to produce what it was designed to produce. The seed contains your destiny. As a seed, I carry the blueprint for my life.

> Are they Hebrews? So am I. Are they Israelites? So am I. Are they the seed of

> Abraham? So am I. (2 Corinthians 11:22)

Since my life is a seed, I shouldn't consider my life as it is now. My future is different. A seed provides a way for us to see beyond the confined or restrictive boundaries that we see around us. I should be able to see growth and hope that's attached to my life. The future of a seed is meant to be bigger and better than its present limitations. Regardless of size or appearance, there is multiplication and harvest that's ahead of us. Once the seed of faith is planted in your heart, you are a new creation. Your destiny is set, and your old life passes away.

> Therefore, if anyone is in Christ, he is a new creation; old things have passed away; behold, all things have become new (2 Corinthians 5:17)

The seed has done nothing and yet it has everything. Contained within a seed is the DNA for its destiny. As the world tries to deal with me in the way that it dealt with Jesus, I should know as much as Jesus did. Victory is in my DNA. *"Your eyes saw my substance, being yet unformed. And in Your book they all were written..."* Psalm 139:16. Even when nothing else is predictable around me, my future is predictable because every seed carries the power to produce what it was designed to produce. We aren't a product of university grades or some doctor's prognosis. My future is tied to what God has already placed in my heart.

> But God gives it a body as He pleases,
> and to each seed its own body
> (1 Corinthians 15:38)

I am not going to change what the seed produces. An apple seed will never produce an orange tree, and an orange tree will never produce a banana. The results are unchangeable. Time or age will never change the results. With fixed outcome 'or vision' in mind, I can approach life with the destiny in mind. I can also stand against anything which has negative impact on the expected result - the fruit, and take advantage of what I was born to be.

> "Before I formed you in the womb I knew you; Before you were born I sanctified you; I ordained you…"
> (Jeremiah 1:5)

At the time of writing this, it is 17 years since I decided to believe in Jesus. But it was only ten years ago when I figured out why I was experiencing more defeats than victories. That's when it also occurred to me that all humans are born winners in the first place. The conception process is the evidence of that fact. Our conception reveals why the odds for us to be in our mother's womb should be celebrated. In that moment, I was among millions that were chasing a single egg. At the end, I was the one who won. Nonetheless, the seed of the winner needed nine months to grow within the boundaries of the mother's womb. My growth will bring into reality the vision of what the creator had in mind.

> The field is the world; the good seed are the children of the kingdom …
> (Matthew 13:38 Kings James Version)

I am now out here on a journey with other winners. This is a journey in which my spirit has taken on the challenge of living within the limitations of my body. However, now you are here, do you still see yourself as a winner? Can we be sure of where we are going? The world doesn't even seem to care about that, does it? The majority of the world's population are far from seeing themselves as winners. Thousands of restrictions have been imposed on our journeys. My work colleague once said, 'I wish I could care less about how I looked!' Well! As born-winners, we can either be distracted by other's opinion or take an opportunity to step into our deserved freedom.

> And the son said to him, '<u>Father, I have sinned</u> against heaven and in your sight, and am no longer worthy to be called your son.' (Luke 15:21)

Sadly, my journey to freedom was surprisingly just like that of the youngster that Jesus called the prodigal or, in other words, 'wasteful'. The prodigal son's thoughts were not so much different from the way people think today. His approach to life has created endless debate, in the press and in the world at large. Read the story in Luke 15:11-32. It wasn't God that had driven the lad into boozing, partying and 3am adventures. This young man had thoughts which weren't founded on any eternal principles. His attraction to short term glory was reminiscent of the economic boom and bust we see today. He overlooked the principle of a seed, time and harvest. He tried to manufacture the fruit of his life. He thought he could be faster, cleverer, and easily grab the headlines. But, as his contemporaries, the prodigal son overlooked the small print.

> But when he had spent all, there arose a severe famine in that land, and he began to be in want (Luke 15:14)

If I were to imagine the events that left the young adventurer devastated, I would be able to see why his willowy and slim lady might have decided to leave. Of course, she couldn't imagine seeing her glowing skin and naturally shiny hair go without the necessary make-up. The lad possibly lived on credit cards for months trying to keep his high maintenance lady in swanky shoes. She may have never missed any must-see shows and intimate gigs in town. Like me, the prodigal son didn't know how to safeguard his investments against life's occurrences. He didn't know where to invest and where to store the fruit of his labour.

> but lay up for yourselves treasures in heaven, where neither moth nor rust destroys and where thieves do not break in and steal (Matthew 6:20)

However, the prodigal son was smart enough to realize that he had done his best under the circumstances. He realized that he lost control of his life when he left where he belonged. He was like a tree that had been uprooted from a riverbank and planted in the desert. That is why the wannabe hero decided to take the journey back to the starting point – home. He wanted a fresh start. He wanted to become a child again. In a sense, he realized he was born free to live free.

> Stand fast therefore in the liberty by which Christ has made us free, and do not be entangled again… (Galatians 5:1)

My role model is Jesus, the Christ. His life started as a seed. Even though he was born in an animal shed, his future was fixed. He was conceived with an end in mind. Like us, there was nothing he went through that could have changed his destiny. That's why my victory is guaranteed. *...we are more than conquerors through Him...* (Romans 8:37). That is why my love is unconditional. *...because the love of God has been poured out in our hearts...* (Romans 5:5). Once seed of faith is planted where it needs to be planted, our fruit is guaranteed.

We can feel small and insignificant because less of our potential is released. Maybe none whatsoever is yet to be released into real life. Victory may appear to be distant and far away. A seed may seem to have everything but without an outward impact. I could be tempted to think that there is no answer to my situation. I could be tempted to park my dreams in a garage, lock them up, and pursue something else. However, as a seed, all of the potential is released once I am planted where I need to be planted.

In nature, a caterpillar would live where it can feed-on what it needs to transform into a butterfly. Likewise, the seed for a born again Christian wouldn't just flourish anywhere. For me to conquer the world that I was born to conquer, overcome the circumstances that I was designed to overcome, and secure the victories that I was born to secure, I will need to discover my destiny. I need to be rooted and grounded in a place that I will bear fruit. Like the prodigal son, our lives will turn around when we realize that we weren't invested in the right place.

> The heaven, even the heavens, are the Lord's; But the earth He has given to the children of men (Psalm 115:16)

Your relationship with the World is like that of a ground and a seed. The Earth would receive and accommodate you like a seed. In the manner that the ground accommodates a seed, the world is designed to accommodate us. We were born on the Earth because the Earth was initially the Promised Land. However, Jesus changed everything. As a believer, your heart is now the Promised Land. The seed is the means by which the heavens exploit the conditions of your heart.

> Do not be deceived, God is not mocked; for whatever a man sows, that he will also reap (Galatians 6:7)

The transformation starts once the seed has fallen to the ground – the heart. Intimacy develops as long as the seed stays in the ground. It is like marriage. My life depends on how the relationship between the seed and the ground develops. Initially, nothing is obvious to those who are around us. All the important transactions and interactions are hidden. Roots negotiated their way around rocks and pebbles as they hold on to what would enables us to come off the ground. If the connection between the Word of God as a seed and our hearts as the ground isn't disrupted, something good will come off the ground and our lives will start to bear fruit.

> But others fell on good ground and yielded a crop: some a hundredfold, some sixty, some thirty (Matthew 13:8)

Now I know that if I am going through troubled times, the seed isn't the problem. The seed is incorruptible. *"Having been born again, not of corruptible seed but incorruptible, through the word of God which lives and abides forever"* 1 Peter 1:23. If I only take the seed into account, I am by design supposed to be healthy, wealthy and prosperous. God's plan for me is incorruptible. It will never change. But the seed could be dormant. The wheat seeds taken from the hand of a mummy in an Egyptian pyramid were grown in England 3000 years later. Hence, a seed is limited to the conditions it sits on. If we want success, we may need to look at the conditions in which our seed grows. The condition of my heart will affect the outcome. It decides how much fruit my life produces. If we want to be prosperous, we will need to ensure that our hearts can produce abundance. If we can take the limits off our hearts, the sky is the limit.

We have an identity

(2 Corinthians 5:17)

▽

We are incorruptible – the seed

(1 Peter 1:23)

▽

We've a home

– the heart

2

WOMB

- Your Heart is the Womb -

My journey started when the seed of faith was planted in my heart. It started when God declared freedom to the place that shapes my life – my heart. My heart is the womb because that's where my life is fashioned. When we receive Jesus, God doesn't promise to show up in our physical senses or feelings. He shows up in our hearts. The mighty one has chosen to live in my heart. The destination for every blessing is in my heart. What the Old Testament called the *Promised Land* is now on the inside of me. That's where the wall of

Jericho needs to come tumbling down. That is where Goliath needs to be taken out. That's where my enemies' influence is diminished. That's where I can access and see the fulfilment of my dreams and aspirations. As you dig deep into your heart you will know why Jesus said that *'the kingdom of God is within you'*.

> Neither shall they say, Lo here! or, lo there! for, behold, the kingdom of God is within you (Luke 17:21 KJV)

Israelites knew that the Messiah 'Christ' was coming to establish the kingdom. The kingdom is what produces everything we need. That's why the disciples asked Jesus …*"Lord, will You at this time restore the kingdom to Israel?"* (Acts 1:6) That's when Jesus made it clear that, what he was sent to establish was not an outward kingdom. My life isn't going to be much influenced by what happens on the outside or by what people think about me.

The kind of journey that the Israelites took from Egypt to the Promised Land is now an inward journey. Once the seed of faith was planted in my heart, I began to reap what was becoming a reality on the inside. The kingdom changes what happens in our hearts.

> Keep your heart with all diligence, For out of it spring the issues of life
> (Proverbs 4:23)

My heart is a nation. That's my Promised Land. There are a lot of similarities between what the Bible calls the Promised Land in the Old Testament and the kingdom that Jesus has placed in your heart. If you want to understand what it takes to live a life you were born to live, look at how the Israelites entered and settled in the Promised Land. Their journey shows that my freedom from bondage and affliction is one thing. Ultimately, it will take courage and boldness for me to deal with anything that has gained influence in my heart. It will take courage for every one of us to enjoy what God has already made available to us.

> Have I not commanded you? Be strong and of good courage; do not be afraid, nor be dismayed, for the Lord your God is with you wherever you go." (Joshua 1:9)

I am called an overcomer because there is something to overcome. *"He who overcomes shall inherit all things…"* (Revelation 21:7). I am a conqueror because there is a world to occupy and conquer. *"Yet in all these things we are more than conquerors…"* (Romans 8:37). I was reminded what happened when the Israelites didn't want to face the challenges they had to face in the Promised Land. They got stuck in the wilderness! *…Our brethren have discouraged our hearts, saying, "The people are greater and taller than we; the cities are great and fortified* *up to heaven…"* (Deuteronomy 1:28). Fear kept them in the wilderness. I only fail if I fail to deal with what is already rooted and grounded in my heart. Then, I wouldn't be able to obtain victories and experience real freedom.

> For "whoever calls on the name of the Lord shall be saved." (Romans 10:13)

When I gave my heart to Jesus, I didn't know that I would still have some challenges. I was like an Israelite who didn't expect to face challenges in the Promised Land. The nonfactual, habitual, and ritual things which occupied my heart were like the giants which occupied the Promised Land. Even though God provided ownership, the Israelites weren't only supposed to occupy the Promised Land, they needed to conquer it. We are not born to occupy the earth, but live to conquer it. The terrifying feeling that came with that responsibility kept the Israelites from having the freedom they deserve.

> but now our whole being is dried up; there is nothing at all except this **manna** before our eyes! (Numbers 11:6)

In the period between 2003 and 2009, I didn't know what it took to occupy and conquer the Promised Land. Like Israelites, I was possibly still eating 'manna' in the wilderness. I went through the most boring period of my Christian life. There is not much excitement when it comes to life in the wilderness. Manna is the name of the food that fell directly from heaven. The Israelites ate manna for breakfast, manna for lunch, and manna for dinner. The question, 'What are you going to have for dinner tomorrow?' was irrelevant. Like a child in a crib, they had to live in a protected place and eat the same thing over and over again for 40 years. None of those who were lucky enough to enter the Promised Land ever claimed to have missed the life or what they ate in the wilderness.

> I fed you with milk and not with solid food; for until now you were not able to receive it, and even now you are still not able (1 Corinthians 3:2)

In a nutshell, the Corinthians (verse above) were in a situation that was similar to the Israelites in the wilderness. Apostle Paul basically told the Corinthians 'if you live under the influence of your physical senses and circumstances, you are no different from babies'. Your life is isolated from the real world just like babies. You will spend a significant amount of time in a protected place such as a crib or cot just like the Israelites in the wilderness. You will have milk for breakfast, milk for lunch and milk for dinner. Like the Israelites who ate manna in the wilderness, your blessing will come as a supernatural provision. You will have no part to play in its appearance. In fact, if our spiritual life is a bit boring, we are possibly having milk for breakfast, milk for lunch and milk for dinner. However, life in the Promised Land will be exciting. You will not be sustained by the same miracle (i.e. manna) day after day and year after year.

> I will give you a new heart and put a new spirit within you; I will take the heart of stone out of your flesh and give you a heart of flesh (Ezekiel 36:26)

For us to dwell where heroes dwell, we will need the heart that heroes have. For us to accomplish what we were born to accomplish, we will need to have the blueprint and building blocks for our new lives. God does not only provide the seed, he provides the heart that allows our blessings to be rooted and grounded – the heart of flesh. He has provided a land … *'flowing with milk and honey,' the glory of all lands* (Ezekiel 20:6). Hence, everything changes because my heart is changed. That is why the children of Israel were commanded to completely remove all the inhabitants of the land. In the New Covenant, Jesus said "*...no one puts new wine into old wineskins…*" (Mark 2:22), because "*…if anyone is in Christ, he is a new creation…*" (2 Corinthians 5:17). Renewal starts from the moment we receive Jesus.

> …the inward man is being renewed day by day (2 Corinthians 4:16)

There is nothing that is needed in a nation that isn't needed in my heart. The kingdom that is within me requires a completely new infrastructure *…that the man of God may be perfect, thoroughly furnished* (2 Timothy 3:17 KJV). Like any nation, I will need people, immigration & border control, law, police, an army, TV/radio station, fire stations, treasury/accounting, language, supreme court, economy, healthcare and national anthem among many other things. Let's look at how an investment on a few of these can change our lives. Since the Promised Land is in my heart, God wants to provide a thoroughly furnished infrastructure.

> …who came in by stealth to spy out our liberty which we have in Christ Jesus, that they might bring us into bondage Galatians 2:4

As a nation, my heart has boundaries. Hence, I will need immigration and border control, so that I can dictate what goes in and out of my life. A lot can go wrong for those who do not acknowledge their boundaries. Countless things could go wrong once I have given an entry clearance or enter into covenant with those who were not meant to be part of my life.

Unsupervised boundaries allow what can terrorize our lives to easily get into our territories. It allows situations which can hurt us to get close. *"Blessed is the man Who walks not in the counsel of the ungodly..."* (Psalm 1:1). It allows other's failures to come in and burden our lives. That's why good nations tend to build relationships with nations which have good border control. Good boundaries enable us to be a faithful custodian of the treasure that God has placed in our lives.

> ... "Who told you that you were naked?"
> ...(Genesis 3:11)

Like TV and radio stations, my heart does broadcast. My life is influenced by what dominates my airwaves. What is being broadcasted in my heart will have more impact on my life than what is being broadcasted in the world around me. *"For from within, out of the heart of men, proceed evil [or good] thoughts..."* Mark 7:21 (brackets mine). My heart's meditation is a broadcast. Everything I speak has to be broadcasted into my heart first "...*For out of the abundance of the heart his mouth speaks*" (Luke 6:45). That's why God asked Adam and Eve the question "*who told you that you were naked?*" (verse above). He didn't ask, 'why did you say you were naked?' There is no record of Satan or anybody telling Adam and Eve that they were naked. In fact, they were the only human beings on the face of the earth. The question seems to suggest that, Adam and Eve's inner broadcast were under siege. The enemy had taken over their airwaves. The direction of our lives changes from the moment we start to dictate what is spoken into our hearts. Everything changed when we start to enforce the broadcast-rights that Jesus redeemed for us.

> ...Casting down *imaginations*, and every high thing that exalteth itself against the knowledge of God, and bringing into

captivity *every thought* to the obedience of Christ (2 Corinthians 10:5 KJV)

We need to build a police force because there are some inner conflicts to resolve and thoughts to bring into captivity. I need to police my mind and thought-life because whatever finds a way into my heart changes something! Without a police force, my heart would be vulnerable because our thought-life is constantly under attack. I need 'police officers' who are easy to identify and call to action. I also need to know their address so that I can easily call them into action. The Bible gives account of what needs to be taken captive and what needs to be set free! It provides the way for me to deal with thoughts which illegally find their way into my territory. For example, if our hearts encounter condemnation, we can call Romans 8:1, *"There is therefore now no condemnation to those who are in Christ Jesus…"* A condemning thought needs to be replaced with an encouraging thought. If fear enters in, we can call 2 Timothy 1:7, *"For God has not given us a spirit of fear, but of power and of love…"* Our well-armed police force will help to remove any confusion that has found its way into our hearts, and protect us from whatever can steal our love, joy and peace.

> Put on the whole armor of God…
> (Ephesians 6:11)

In addition to our border patrol and police, we need an army. Nations do face wars. My heart can be invaded. While borders keep me from those who want to sneak in, an army will stand against any deliberate and purposeful invasion. Our hearts provide a place for us to be militant because there are also some territories to be taken back. The inhabitants of the Promised Land didn't volunteer to go. My physical or emotional problems wouldn't volunteer to go. The following armour is for those who want to build their army and experience long term freedom. The Bible offers a good choice of armour or weapons. Our fully proven and tested armour is listed in Ephesians 6:14-18 *"…having girded your waist with TRUTH, having put on the breastplate… taking the shield of FAITH… And take the helmet of salvation… and the sword of the spirit… PRAYING always".* That's what is needed for me to launch an effective operation and attack the enemy with military precision.

> Beloved, I wish above all things that thou may **prosper**… (3 John 1:2 KJV)

My heart is a nation that is also created for wealth, not poverty. But my wealth isn't going to mysteriously fall from heaven! My heart's economy rests on very different foundations. I reap what I have planted. *"Do not be deceived, God is not mocked; for whatever a man sows, that he will also reap"* (Galatians 6:7). I reap the fruit of my labour. *"Who plants a vineyard and does not eat of its fruit?"* (1 Corinthians 9:7). My economy is based on what God has already given unto me. *"And to one he gave five talents, to another two, and to another one, to each according to his own ability…"* (Matthew 25.15). I prosper as I become a faithful steward of earthly and heavenly treasures that God has already placed in my life.

> Beloved, I wish above all things that
> thou may prosper and **be in *health*…**
> (3 John 1:2 KJV)

For us to be in good health, we needed health insurance. Our hearts need health insurance because even a good nation can face storms. Health threats are like storms. Storms do not discriminate. Storms aren't the one to blame. Jesus used a parable to show us why the storms do come, on both the person who's built their house on the sand, and the one who's built their house on the rock. So, why do bad things happen to good people? According to Jesus, good people are prepared. Even those who have a very good infrastructure (i.e. good police force and good border control) need to be prepared! *"Be sober, be vigilant; because your adversary the devil walks about like a roaring lion, seeking whom he may devour"* (1 Peter 5:8). What we 'BELIEVE' is an insurance against any kind of health threat.

> For which of you, intending to build a tower, does not sit down first and count the cost, whether he has enough to finish it— (Luke 14:28)

Your nation will also have some accounting responsibility. This is a kind of accounting which will take your heart into another level of spiritual maturity. It is accounting that will set a path for your spiritual maturity. For example, when Jesus multiplied five loaves and two fish, the Bible says, *"So they all ate and were filled, and twelve baskets of the leftover fragments were taken up by them"* (Luke 9:17). They didn't just say 'we had a lot of left-overs!' They counted! The spiritual world is, by nature sensitive to numbers *"…the very hairs of your head are all numbered…"* (Luke 12:7). Our spiritual life will be influenced by our accounting practices. That is why the disciples of Jesus needed to know the scale of each miracle.

When Jesus rose from the dead, he went to the sea of Tiberias and helped his disciples to catch fish. *And He said to them, "Cast the net on the right side of the boat, and you will find some."* (John 21:6). *"Simon Peter went up and dragged the net to land, full of large fish, <u>one hundred and fifty-three</u>..."* (John 21:11). In the excitement of catching-up with someone who has just risen from the dead, most of us would have just said 'we caught a lot of fish!' However, the path to my spiritual maturity requires me to learn to account for what is happening in my life. In the kingdom, we do not only do accounting before starting a project, we continuously take account of what God is doing in our lives. We monitor the impact of our salvation. We account for every one of our blessings. God is equally taking account of every heart that has been set free.

> And he did evil, because he did not prepare his heart to seek the Lord (2 Chronicles 12:14)

If we want to face the world with a supernatural confidence, we will need to prepare. Heaven, health, and wealth are ready for those who are prepared. We cannot fail! We can only fail to prepare our hearts. That is why Jesus said *"Listen! Behold, a sower went out to sow"* (Mark 4:3). There is nothing that can truly transform or come into our lives by accident. Hence, it is not Godly to think we can never know what is around the corner. We can determine what is going to happen tomorrow. We can face what we are prepared for. Jesus repeatedly referred to the fact that '*it is written*!' The blueprint for building my life is already written. We can learn to plant what is written into our hearts.

> A good man out of the good treasure of his heart brings forth good; and an evil man out of the evil treasure of his heart brings forth evil… (Luke 6:45)

Until recently, I never thought of my heart as a place that's much bigger. What was in my imagination was a little room with a little chair that God could hardly sit on comfortably. I thought, if God could ever live in my heart, He will be very uncomfortable. Whenever I made comments such as 'this or that thing has changed my heart!' I was generalizing about what's happened in a small part of a huge infrastructure. I never visualized my heart as a kingdom. Now I know that my world is much bigger. I can grow beyond the boundaries that I have set around my heart.

> being confident of this very thing, that He who has begun a good work in you will complete it until the day of Jesus Christ (Philippians 1:6)

To Jesus, my heart is like the place that was initially given to the children of Abraham. But circumstances led them to abandon their inheritance. Like Israelites, I couldn't foresee victory because I believed the place I had abandoned 'my heart' was infested and fortified. However, if my heart is the Promised Land, I need to take the journey back to where I belong. Unlike the children of Israel who thought they were better off in Egypt; I should know that I am not better off in the world. I cannot just go to school, get good grades, and then find a safe and secure job. To God, the Promised Land was flowing with milk and honey. That's what God sees in the hearts of those he has redeemed. Your heart is flowing with milk and honey. That is the way God sees the hearts of those who have given their life to Jesus. He cannot wait to see the magical transformation which begins once we have embraced His freedom and become spiritual infants.

3

INFANT

- magical transformation -

The Bible says, a child was born. His name was Jesus. He was not the biological son of Joseph. God is the one who provided the seed. Jesus was the Son of God, born of a virgin. But God said to Joseph, if you take Mary to be your wife, and raise the child, He will become your son. The Son of God will become the son of man. He will be called the son of David because Joseph was the descendant of King David. So, we become children of the one who will raise us up. I became a son of God when I allowed God to transform my heart. I became a son of the person I have allowed to influence *my character and nature.* Practically, we become sons or daughters of God once we are imparted with *his nature and character.*

> Behold what manner of love the Father has bestowed on us, that we should be called children [teknon] of God! …
> (1 John 3:1)

There are a number of words for 'child' or 'son' in the Greek language. The one commonly used is TEKNON, which means "child in relation to parentage". *They answered and said to Him [Jesus], "Abraham is our father"* … (John 8:39). They had ancestry connection to Abraham. The other word – HUIOS, means "a child with regard to displaying nature and character". *"Abraham is our father",* the Jews replied. Jews believed that their identity and future was tied to the promises that were made to

Abraham. "*If you were Abraham's children,*" Jesus pointed out to them, "*you would do the works of Abraham*" (John 8:39). When I received Jesus as my Lord and Saviour, I started my relationship with God as an infant. As a child of God, I will manifest a character and life that resembled God.

> For as many as are led by the Spirit of God, these are sons [huios] of God (Romans 8:14)

Raising a child is a giant undertaking. According to the Bible, a spiritual child or a *teknon* is born. However, being born is one thing. When I was born, my dad did possibly call me his son, and in my sister's case his daughter. But it is by faith that a parent would call their newly born child their son or daughter. We eventually become daughters or sons '*huios*' of the one who has raised us up. My parents could have chosen to give me up for adoption, or for somebody else to raise me.

A born-again Christian '*huios*' relates to God with an affectionate intimacy, privy to His saving council, and obedient to His will. Jesus provided a way for a spiritual child 'teknon' to be transformed into a son or daughter 'huios'.

> …"Assuredly, I say to you, unless you are converted and become as little children, you will by no means enter the kingdom of heaven (Matthew 18:3)

Jesus received all of his disciples as children. He told his followers that unless they are willing to be like children, they cannot enter the Kingdom of heaven. He addressed his disciples as children when possibly some of them were older 'age wise' than him. They were called 'disciples' because they allowed Jesus' character and nature to transform their hearts from the state of spiritual infancy. We abandon the growth we have had in the flesh and become infants again. That is an opportunity which

God is giving us when we start our relationship with Him. Our status change from the moment we believe. Once we have accepted Jesus, we become infants, and God takes the responsibility of a father.

> Jesus asked his disciples, "Children, have you got any food"? ... (John 21:5 paraphrased, also see John 13:33 and Mark 10:24)

Disciples of Jesus were adults who gave their life to him. But Jesus received them as *teknon* or a child. As spiritual infants, they seem to have had a completely different nature and character. They were shocked by miracles, and most of the time they were amazed and terrified by Jesus' approach to things. Most of the time they were anxious and fearful. They even ran away from Him when He was going to be nailed to the cross. They followed Jesus, but they weren't bold. There was also no sign whatsoever that one day they would be transformational or be as bold as Jesus. Then, they witnessed supernatural transformation.

> …Do not marvel that I said to you,
> 'You must be born again.' (John 3:3-7)

The term 'born-again' has gained recognition in Christian circles all over the world. Over centuries, this life-changing experience has had a number of other expressions such as salvation, becoming a believer, or coming into faith etc. There are millions of people who are responding to its eternal benefits or eternal life. Nonetheless, its true relevance for our life on the earth is still unknown to many. Masses are missing out on its earth-bound benefits. Eternal life isn't solely for those who want to be celebrities in heaven. It's also for those who would like to live by faith and see real victories on earth.

Nothing equals the abundance of life that comes with the born-again experience. As *huios*, you grow differently from the person you have already grown to be. You aren't going to be the same person doing something different. The experience is more than a fresh start or a new beginning to your earthbound life. This time, you aren't growing to get old and die. You're rather growing to live.

> "I will be a Father to you, And you shall be My sons [huios] and daughters, Says the Lord Almighty" (2 Corinthians 6:18)

So, when I received Jesus, I was given a life that I could take advantage of. I was a *teknon* who was endowed with power which would enable me to become a son/daughter of God – *huios*. The creation awaits that transformation. I can either seize that opportunity and grow or ignore it and live as an infant. Unlike birth, which is a momentary experience, we do not become a *huios* in a day. A spiritual infant will grow at the speed that they are responding to Jesus – the Word of God.

> as newborn babes, desire the pure milk of the word, that you may grow thereby (1 Peter 2:2)

Those who are being fed the right thing, they are being fed an incorruptible food. We are feasting on what *lives and abides forever.* It all stays in! There are no waste pipes in heaven. Every bit of the good snack we have eaten stays in! There will be no need to go to the toilet once we have had the pure milk of the Word of God. Spiritual infants who are well-fed will become toddlers.

4

TODDLER

- take Step by Step -

A spiritual toddler is what I would call a born-again Christian who has started to take some steps into their liberty. We are toddlers because we aren't stagnant, we are toddling. It is not the age that makes us toddlers. It is the steps we are taking. God kind of faith will never be alone, it will always have actions. Our initial steps may be erratic and inconsistent. We can for a period have steps which aren't even or regular in pattern. Our journeys may seem to be unpredictable and filled with uncertainty. However, in the heart and mind of every toddler is the word 'freedom'. We are simply stepping into our liberty.

> Now I say that the heir, as long as he is a child, does not differ at all from a slave, though he is master of all
> (Galatians 4:1)

God wouldn't like us to spend our whole life as infants. That's because as long as an heir is a child, she/he are legally incapable of taking full advantage of what is rightfully hers/his. However, a child or an infant that is being fed properly will have no difficulty evolving into a toddler. A child of God will evolve into a toddler. As toddlers, we are taking some steps to overcome the limitations we had as baby Christians. This transformation is important because a child, or a minor, is incapable of any valid act in a legal sense. We take steps which will enable us to experience what we never experienced as newly born-again Christians.

> Thus also faith by itself, if it does not have works, is dead (James 2:17)

For an infant to become a toddler, they need more than the word of God. This stage of growth isn't solely based on what we are being fed. Toddlers are those who have discovered that food isn't all they need. At this stage, we need more than day and night of additional feeds on the word of God. Toddlers' revelation goes beyond food and sleep. The word of God isn't all that's needed for us to become spiritual toddlers. From this point forward, our liberty depends on our response to what is revealed to us. As toddlers, growth is based on our actions. For example, there isn't any good nutritious food that can enable us to ride a bicycle. As spiritual toddlers, we are step by step, taking actions that would enable us to overcome the barriers that keep us from experiencing the *glorious liberty* of the children of God.

> … into the *glorious liberty* of the children of God (Romans 8:21)

It is step by step adventure. These are steps of the one who's never walked before. We are stepping from one *freedom* to another. Toddler's steps aren't dictated by what those who are around them can see, they are influenced by what they themselves can see. They are moved by what is revealed to them. *"The steps of a good man are ordered by the Lord…"* Psalm 37:23. We are gaining exposure to the world which needs to be reached and explored. Regardless of all the missed steps and tumbles, toddlers will, by nature, press on. Our imperfect steps are taking us out of our comfort zone. Those who desire growth will take steps regardless of how correct those steps are. As a spiritual toddler, you take steps which enable you to experience more of what God has placed on the inside of you.

> …those who by reason of use have *their senses exercised* to discern both good and evil (Hebrews 5:14)

These are steps which will also enable us to exercise our senses. Our spiritual sensibility to what surrounds us is heightened as we toddle. We start to see things we have never seen before. Step by step, we are reaching out to something that our senses are made aware of. "…*the eyes of your understanding being enlightened*" (Ephesians 1:18). We will toddle even more and more as we experience the world that surrounds us. We will keep on discovering the steps we need to take and the direction in which we need to move to, to experience life in ways we have not experienced before.

> Now faith is the *substance of things* hoped for, the evidence of things not seen (Hebrews 11:1)

For a toddler, toys are a *substance of things* that they will see in real life. They are a window or picture of the things a toddler will hope to see in real life. Toys introduce a child to what they will see in the future. They make it easy for toddlers to understand the kind of world they will encounter. Even though toys are unrealistic or imaginary, they give us an opportunity to picture the world in a small way. They are a *substance of things* hoped for, and the evidence of things not seen. If what happens in real life is spiritual, what happens in the physical life is a parable. Toys and physical life are a representation, just like the parables which Jesus taught. Toddlers are given a glimpse of the world that's beyond their physical reach.

> And He said to them, "Do you not understand this parable? How then will

> you understand all the parables?
> (Mark 4:13)

Jesus used parables to show how physical things and circumstances can help us to understand the spiritual world. For toddlers, toys provide a picture of the world they will encounter as they grow up. Just like toys, physical environment provides a picture of what we will face in the spiritual realm. Even though we are exposed to what we can see, touch, smell, taste and hear, we can start to think beyond what we can relate to. As spiritual toddlers, the steps we take help us to relate what is in the physical world and prepare us for what is in the spiritual world. The physical world provides a mirror of what God is relaying to us.

> Jesus said to them, "My food is to do [ACTION] the will of Him who sent Me, and to finish His work (John 4:34 brackets mine)

Toddlers have an awareness that they cannot crawl to their destiny. They can see where they need to go, and they know that crawling isn't going to get them there. We can't settle for the safety of crawling. With a world to be reached, we don't want to be classified as infants or be classified as vulnerable for the rest of our lives. We are going to make every effort to *overcome* our limitations and take our freedom. Even if our bottoms hit the floor a few times, we wouldn't settle for the short-term benefits of crawling. Crawling isn't going to deliver the results we need. We will stand up and press on. Even at this stage, toddlers can compare our short-term pain to our long-term gains. As spiritual toddlers, we can foresee freedom. We can see opportunities for breakthrough. Step by step, we are reaching out to everything God has placed within our reach.

> For we walk by faith, not by sight
> (2 Corinthians 5:7)

A Christian's life is described as a walk of faith. The "walk" of a believer signifies one's behaviour, conduct, lifestyle and manner of life. In Romans chapter eight, the Apostle Paul presents a specific way that those who are willing to grow can walk in life. The chapter starts, *"There is therefore now no condemnation to those who are in Christ Jesus, who **do not walk** according to the flesh, but according to the Spirit"* (Romans 8:1).

There is no condemnation, censure, criticism, castigation, stricture, denunciation, damnation, or vilification from God. As spiritual toddlers, we learn to progressively allow our freedom to be influenced by the promptings of the Holy Spirit. We become very much aware that we aren't the only ones who walk about. *"Be sober, be vigilant; because your adversary* **the devil walks about** *like a roaring lion, seeking whom he may devour"* (1 Peter 5:8). Hence, a child of God will walk by faith.

5

CHILD

- Vulnerability to Idols -

From the moment your child-like steps take you in the right direction, you will bump into idols. You will step in the world which is currently immersed in social media and reality television. It is the world in which it is hard to ignore the call of those who seek to be our idols. Throughout the media, their call has actually grown louder and louder. They know that there's something more important to satisfy in you than physical human needs like food, water, and shelter. They aren't visually impaired. If your heart is the Promised Land, they can see your prime spot.

They can see an empty seat of honour in your heart and they want to go for it! In fact, God has created such a place in the heart of every human being. The world's idols know that there is a desire to connect within each one of us, to be inspired and to be an inspiration to others. They want to take advantage of the realm of influence you have over all those that connect with you. This is the revelation which has given an exceptional voice to those who seek and desire fame.

> …For you are the temple of the living God. As God has said: "I will dwell in them And walk among them…"
> (2 Corinthians 6:16)

However, it took a bit of time for me to realize that I don't have a choice on whether I have an idol or not. Our hearts can't exist without one. Whether we like it or not, we'll find it difficult to survive without one. There's always someone we want to be like. Actually, no human on the face of the earth has ever survived without the inspiration, motivation, or leadership of an idol. They may pick from one of those exalted by their world or one of those they're trying to be or to impress. Whatever we call them – our boss, our mum, our aunt, the kid next door or Big Daddy; there is always someone to be crazy about out there. Regardless of a person's age or gender, there is a constant requirement for direction, course and leadership. That's why 'sheep' are a picture that's chosen by Jesus to express humanity's need for a shepherd.

> "My sheep hear My voice, and I know them, and they follow Me" said Jesus (John 10:27)

Most of our celebrities may not be our idols, meaning, not idolised. An Idol (noun) is an image or representation of a god used as an object of worship. Synonyms are: icon, god, image, likeness, fetish, totem, statue, figure, figurine, doll, carving. An idol could also be a person or thing that is greatly admired, loved, or revered. It could be a person who is recognized in their own field - a famous person, perhaps in entertainment or sport (for example an Olympic medal swimmer). Those who are celebrities may turn out to be our idols.

> …children, keep yourselves from idols.
> Amen (1 John 5:21)

It's now many years since I idolised Bob Marley. I embraced his message and sang his music like they were words direct from a god. My heart was so immersed, and so influenced by him that I started to adopt his political and social views. This immersion showed itself by the clothes I wore, the hat I put on my head, the way I walked and the dance I adopted. I started to match my lifestyle into his lifestyle. I was among many that were reached by Bob Marley's powerful influence across cultures.

> Don't put your confidence in powerful people; there is no help for you there. When they breathe their last, they return to the earth, and all their plans die with them (Psalms 146:3-4 New Living Translation)

Although Bob Marley seemed to deserve all the plaudits he won, there was a line that took forever for me to cross. The fact is, I couldn't smoke cannabis or grow dreadlocks. That's because I had another idol – my dad. So, having Bob Marley, my dad, and the creator, left me with a bit of a personality mix up. Some personalities can be so different in nature that they can't co-exist peacefully within you. My mishmash of idols over time became the source of incoherent thoughts, contradictory statements, inconsistent outcomes, and obviously, some interesting hindsight. In any turn of events, what may have been a whisper of discontent grew louder and eventually develop into a sense of turmoil. However, my world turned around when I identified a set of 'idols' that worked for me.

> … truly our fellowship is with the Father, and with his Son Jesus Christ
> (1 John 1:3)

Do you want to know why you'll honour what your idols honour and celebrate what they celebrate? You'll buy what you think they're buying and eat what you think they're eating? You'll love what they love and hate what they hate? Eventually, you will become a servant to their logic. In fact, millions of newspapers and magazines are sold every day because we need something to keep their image vivid and alive within us. That's why we can't help but wear their jumper, t-shirt, cap, onesie and pants. The truth is that, our hearts are in *bondage* to what we have identified ourselves with. And what's more, further examination will help us to know whether the idol we are identifying ourselves with is what is causing us problems or providing a solution.

> Do you not know that to whom you present yourselves slaves to obey, you are that one's slaves… (Romans 6:16)

As we'll see, one of the facts that deserves more attention in this idol phenomenon is that we're not the one in control. Our idols set the standard because they are what we aspire to be. You'll easily see things the way your choice idol or hero sees them. As time goes on, it'll become more and more likely for our hearts to respond in the way that we believe our idol would respond. *Now when they saw the boldness of Peter and John, and perceived that they were uneducated and untrained men, they marveled. And they realized that they had been with Jesus* (Acts 4:13). If our idol fears uncertainty, we're not likely to be different. If they are using drugs and profanity to deal with their frustration, we can find ourselves doing the same. I mean, the choices we make when we are up against the wall will be affected. We'll easily react to our circumstances in a way that doesn't solve problems. That's why the Jews couldn't help but join the Pharisees in the shout –*Crucify him*!

> He who walks with wise men will be wise… (Proverbs 13:20)

Whether we agree with this or not, there's a marriage between me and my idol because my statement to my idol is simply this, …*I would rather be who you are; I wish I could live in your company daily; I wish what was yours could be mine; I would love your identity to be my identity, your god to be my god, and your pain to be my pain* (Ruth 1:16-17 paraphrased). In a spiritual sense, I am sold into the circumstances of my idol. I am literally saying "If you can do it, I possibly could. If you couldn't do it, I couldn't possibly do it!". The consequences can either be good or bad. The process is supernatural in many ways.

> Do you not know that to whom you present yourselves slaves to obey, you are that one's slaves whom you obey, whether of sin leading to death, or of obedience leading to righteousness? (Roman 6:16)

Let's face it! Replacing your idol changes everything, because there's an idol behind everything. Every action that has affected human life, started with people who had to believe in a particular leadership. Every divorce, abortion, addiction, stress, and act of greed has an origin because people tend to respond to leadership of any sort. That's why the nation of Germany once believed in Hitler. On the other hand, every birth, launch, journey, promotion, goal, and victory also has an origin. You can call it: generosity, health, love, peace, liberty, industry or creative enterprise; they all have inspiration. That's why Jesus declared that anyone who believes in him will be able to do what he did.

> "Most assuredly, I say to you, he who believes in Me, the works that I do he will do also; and greater works than these he will do… (John 14:12)

So, if you want to speed up victory in someone's life, ensure they have the right set of influencers behind them. Those influencers may be seated in heaven … *When the Lord Jesus had finished talking with them, he was taken up into heaven and sat down in the place of honor at God's right hand* (Mark

16:19 KJV) or active on earth. Regardless of their geographic or virtual location, they can still impact our standard of living. Sir Isaac Newton once put it this way, "If I have seen further, it is by standing on the shoulders of giants". The great scientists like Albert Einstein and Isaac Newton didn't pick up the baton from leaders who were fictional. They didn't pick up from people who exploit the personal branding or perception programming that we see today. To see victory, we may need to stand behind the people who have made a real difference in the world.

> "And He spoke a parable to them:
> "Can the blind lead the blind? Will they
> not both fall into the ditch?" said Jesus
> (Luke 6:39)

Jesus was born in a nation which had failed to deal with its dodgy celebrities. As such, Jesus came across image-engineering at its best. He was raised in the nation of Israel which had religious leaders Pharisees and Sadducees who used their influence to limit the people's freedom and liberty. Just as today, Jewish celebrities were given an enormously important role – probably the most important role in determining society's direction and progress. However, they used their status to ruin the lives of many people. The Jews had repeatedly allowed the beliefs of their chosen celebrities to lead them into a desperate situation. Nearly three million Jews had previously allowed the judgement and beliefs of as few as eight people to keep them wandering in the desert for 40 years. Unlike the religious Pharisees, Jesus had a liberating vision for his followers.

> Stand fast therefore in the liberty by which Christ has made us free…
> (Galatians 5:1)

Most of the world's idols do whatever needs to be done to present themselves favourably and make you feel like you are having a piece of their cake. Unlike Jesus, they would hire PR teams to exaggerate or distort vital clues to their real identity. But what is going to change your life isn't what you think about your idol, but what your idol genuinely thinks about you. *For I know the thoughts that I think toward you, saith the LORD, thoughts of peace, and not of evil, to give you an expected end* (Jeremiah 29:11 KJV). Jesus had an unfavourable response to people who branded themselves in a way that only exploits people's hearts.

> …woe to you, scribes and Pharisees, hypocrites! For you shut up the kingdom of heaven against men; for you neither go in yourselves, nor do you allow those who are entering to go in (Matthew 23:13).

That is a challenge that comes from living in a world which has celebrities who live to exploit their fans. It is very unfortunate that when it comes to the choice of idol, a lot of us tend to ignore this most important rule of engagement. I repeat – what your idol thinks about you is more important than what you think about them.

> For as he thinks in his heart, so *is* he…
> (Proverbs 23:7)

All idols have huge economic impact. The economic situation in the world today reveals what kind of influence most of us are having today. The celebrity phenomenon can tell us why wealth is in the hands of very few people. It can explain why 90 per cent of the global wealth is in the hands of 10 per cent of the world population (inequality.org). Our access to the unlimited supply of resources we need to live a prosperous life is limited by the people we have idolised. In fact, everything that Jesus said and did would have economic impact on your life. We can stand on the shoulders of someone who has a different approach to wealth.

> "And all Mine are Yours, and Yours are Mine…" said Jesus (John 17:10)

In an ideal situation, your god is your saviour, and your saviour is your god. There is a god behind every celebrity, even when that god isn't obvious to you or them. King David's victory against his enemies relied on this very revelation.

Goliath was a celebrity to his followers. He was the wrong kind of celebrity. Even though nobody else in the Israelite camp saw beyond Goliath's stature, David knew that Goliath's huge stature, status, rants and body armour was not what he should pay attention to. To him, the battle belongs to God.

> Then all this assembly shall know that the Lord does not save with sword and spear; for the battle is the Lord's, and He will give you into our hands."
> (1 Samuel 17:47).

David knew that he could only place Goliath behind Goliath's own god which was a statue. That's where Goliath looked small enough to be defeated. That is where every child of God should place everything that comes against them. David, who was physically disadvantaged, knew that he was significant enough to defeat Goliath because he had Creator God on his side.

> [43] So the Philistine said to David, "Am I a dog, that you come to me with sticks?" And the Philistine [Goliath] cursed David by *his gods*. [45] Then David said to the Philistine, "You come to me with a sword, with a spear, and with a javelin. But I come to you in the name of the Lord of hosts, the God of the armies of Israel, whom you have defied.
> (1 Samuel 17:43/45)

How many idols do we need? The Bible has given an answer which is not simply Mum, Dad, and God. That's because idol is opposite to God or God cannot be idolised. "*…changed the glory of the incorruptible God into an image made like corruptible man…*" (Romans 1:23). In fact, Jesus doesn't want to be our idol. He is calling us into a fellowship. He is inviting you into a very particular communion. You are in a company of three. *Our fellowship is with the Father, and with His Son Jesus Christ* and the Holy Spirit (1 John 1:3). You are set to accomplish much more in this fellowship.

This is the fellowship that will enable us to take full advantage of our childhood. For us to have the freedom we need to decide our own future, we will need to learn how to take full advantage of the mighty influence, resources, and standard of living that this fellowship brings into our lives. Then, we can evolve into spiritual giants and take some new territories.

6

TEEN

- Push Boundaries! -

Although the boundaries of the Promised Land were clearly marked by God, the Israelites only occupied a fraction of the promise. They allowed themselves to be confined in a different set of boundaries. The promise was bigger than what they ever experienced. It is a spiritual picture of what those who are spiritual teenagers try to avoid. As spiritual teenagers, we can sense that there is more to life than what the world avails to us. We lift up our heads, looking out, and climb the walls to reach out to what is beyond our childhood limitations. We would like to access 'all things'.

> "Enlarge the place of your tent…
> Lengthen your cords, And strengthen
> your stakes (Isaiah 54:2)

My teen years were characterized by my effort to redefine my boundaries. It was the season for me to question my boundaries. I wanted to know what it feels like to have no limits. I wanted to break away from childhood limitations. I wanted to experience some of the things 'I believed' were hidden from me. I wanted to try everything and anything I could ever have an opportunity to try. As spiritual teens, we want to have the big picture. If I am no longer a toddler, why can't I go for a proper walk. I do not want to be like the Israelites who limited themselves to a small part of what was available to them. As spiritual teens, we want to go beyond what culture and traditions of man have confined us into. We want to go beyond artificial boundaries of our dwellings and explore the promised land.

> And He has made from one blood every nation of men to dwell on all the face of the earth, and has determined their pre-appointed times and the boundaries of their dwellings
> (Acts 17:26)

Limitations and boundaries are two different things. A child may have difficulties in distinguishing between the two. Boundaries may look like limitations, and limitations may look like boundaries. The enemy will put limitations on our lives. God will set some boundaries to protect our treasures, gifts and freedom. We have property lines. Nations were created for the same reason. Successful people keep '*all things*' within their intended boundaries. Every treasure that God has placed in our lives has designated boundaries. *All things* have perimeters within which they will work together for good.

> And we know that *all things* work together for good to those who love God, to those who are the called according to His purpose
> (Romans 8:36)

At a certain point in our spiritual walk we will become spiritual teenagers. That is when we would challenge the man-made rules and regulations. We would say, 'how comes none of the stuff we see in the Bible are being fulfilled in our lives?' 'Why do a lot of us live below our privileges?' we would argue. Like David, we would question the status quo. Like David, we wouldn't wait until we have gone through institutions, military ranks and religious ordinations. We would challenge the status quo and face Goliath. David could have been as young as 15 years old when he faced Goliath. If the status quo is poor and sick, if the status quo doesn't honour the Word of God, spiritual teenagers will rise to the occasion and take the opportunity to pursue freedom.

> And Saul said to David, "You are not able to go against this Philistine to fight with him; for <u>you are a youth</u>, and he a man of war from his youth."
> (1 Samuel 17:33)

As a child, I grew up with boundaries which gave me a limited access to the world. Those boundaries were not set by me personally. I chose to trust the boundaries which were set by those who had authority over my life. The heir *is under guardians and stewards until the time appointed by the father* (Galatians 4:1-2). I chose to live within the boundaries set by my family, parents, state, and church among others. I consider those boundaries to have been my outer boundaries because they were there waiting for me to grow up enough to understand *all things*. For them to be my boundaries, they will need to be adopted in my heart.

> My little children, for whom I labor in birth again until Christ is formed in you (Galatians 4:19)

A teen is a child who's in a process of transitioning into an adult. We are entering a phase that requires boundaries to be personal. As spiritual teens, we are learning to internalize our boundaries. We internalize that which was once our outer supervision. If the Word of God is to ever provide some boundaries, it will need to find a place in our hearts and minds. It will need to become a personal experience. It will no longer be what my mum, dad or the Bible says, but what I believe. David didn't go with what Jews thought about Goliath, he adopted his own set of beliefs. The devil knows very well that he cannot change what the Bible says, but he can change or challenge what we believe. What spiritual teenagers believe provides the boundaries they need to pursue freedom. What we believe positions us where *all things* are possible.

> Jesus said to him, "If you can believe, *all things* are possible to him who believes." (Mark 9:23)

The devil knows where spiritual teenagers are challenged. Teenagers are vulnerable because they tend to think outside the box. They dare to explore some new territories. The devil knows that the distinction between boundaries and limitations may not be as clear as it should be to them. They are tempted to do things in their own way. As a teenager, I've experienced what happens when I didn't know the difference between boundaries and limitations. I didn't know how keep myself from the chaos that is around the world and keep *all things* within my reach.

> He who did not spare His own Son, but delivered Him up for us all, how shall He not with Him also freely give us *all things*? (Romans 8:32)

I have gone through spiritual childhood and then became a spiritual teenager. I have had boundaries and playthings to use within those boundaries. Boundaries are a blessing. Playthings are a great blessing. However, as teenagers, we begin to have a glimpse of what real things look like because from this point on, we have a little bit more exposure to the real world. From this stage on, we will not interact/engage with shadows, pictures or toys. *Even so we, when we were children, were in bondage under the elements of the world* (Galatians 4:3). Unlike toys and parables which are tangible representations of reality, real world is spiritual. God knows that in the real world, we aren't going to face teddy bears. We are going to face real bears. We are going to face Goliath. What we encounter on a day to day basis will no longer be a parable. Like David, we would no longer tend a few sheep in the hidden fields. Faith places *all things* within our reach.

> The woman said to Him [Jesus], "I know that Messiah is coming" (who is called Christ). "When He comes, He will tell us *all things*" (John 4:25)

The Samaritan woman in the above scripture knew what left her vulnerable to the enemy. She knew why she was repeatedly exposed to the enemy. Like spiritual teenagers, she desired to pursue and experience truth. Even though she wasn't a Jew, she knew what would keep the enemy out of her life. However, many who have read about her encounter with Jesus tend to focus on the negative side of her life. They'd say, "Oh, how bad it is for her to have had six husbands or divorced five times!". Even those who were with

Jesus thought, "how bad it is for our Lord to use his valuable time talking to such a woman!" No one seems to have considered her prophetic insight into life. But she knew something which most people in her world and even those who are going to church today do not know. She knew why the world was failing.

Unlike most people, she didn't attribute her failures to bad childhood, family background or failed marriages. She said, 'I know when the Messiah comes, we will know *all things*'. To her, the answer to her struggles and the struggles of those who were around her was what the Messiah "Jesus" revealed – *all things*. She knew that "all things" will provide her with the boundaries she needed to avoid further disappointments.

> But as it is written: "Eye has not seen, nor ear heard, Nor have entered into

> the heart of man *The things* which God
> has prepared for those who love Him."
> (1 Corinthians 2:9)

The good news is that the Messiah or Jesus did really come, and He did indeed reveal *all things* to those who believed in Him. The Samaritan woman wasn't initially aware of Him. What was once a mystery, unfolded right before her eyes. She was unknowingly talking to the Messiah or Jesus. Even though she was in her sixth marriage, she could no longer consider her shortcomings. She had an opportunity to abandon the boundaries which held her hostage and embrace the boundaries which will set her free. Like most spiritual teenagers, she had already tried everything that her world provided. She had done what she thought she needed to do to stay on track. Then Jesus came and provides the world where *all things* were within her reach.

> But he that lacketh these things is blind, and cannot see afar off… (2 Peter 1:9 KJV)

The subtitle of this chapter is '*push boundaries!*' Some limitations may look like boundaries. There are boundaries or 'limitations' we can push for *all things* to become part of our lives. We can push the boundaries which are holding us hostage. Like spiritual teenagers, we should know that what keeps us from seeing afar off isn't our lack of church attendance or the fact that we were not christened as babies. Our observation of Christmas and Easter seasons will not produce the freedom that we need. *All things* are available to us from the moment we receive Jesus. There is no hidden catch or small print. Like spiritual teenagers, the woman with blood problems in Luke 8:43-48 had some social, cultural, and traditional boundaries to push in order to receive her healing. Spiritual teenagers need to grow in their understanding of *all things*.

> Brethren, do not be children in understanding… (1 Corinthians 14:20)

Spiritual teenagers can be tempted to approach *all things* the way my son (9 years old) approaches all things. Whenever my little boy opened his new toy, he would rush to the play button. The next sentence to come out of his mouth became the familiar; "It doesn't work!" Then, I'll let him know that the toy needed some batteries, and helped him to install them. Then, he would be thrilled. Then, he'd press the next button and then repeat the response; "It still doesn't work!" Then, I will get some directions from the manual and introduce him to a few more things. It is a kind of learning that goes on like that until he eventually becomes aware of *all things*. Jesus doesn't want spiritual teenagers to fiddle their way through life the way that my little boy fiddles with his new toys. All things have a manual – the Bible. With the Holy Spirit within our reach, we have a wealth of truths, training, and personal support.

> Go therefore and make disciples of all
> the nations, …teaching them to observe
> *all things* that I have commanded you…
> (Matthew 28:19-20)

We have very specific commands because *all things* aren't optional. Jesus didn't say, "…if it is okay with you, would you accommodate *all things*. He didn't tell his disciples to offer us whatever suits our circumstances either. He 'commanded' his disciples to 'teach' and not just to preach all things (verse above). Teaching will allow *all things* to be laid in our hearts in a systematic way. *Let all things be done decently and in order…* 1 Corinthians 14:40. In his encounter with Goliath, David didn't have options. He either had what it takes or nothing at all. Goliath wasn't killed by a sling as we would try to imagine. Spiritual teenagers are supposed to *put on the whole armour of God*… Ephesians 6:11-18. Anything short of what Jesus provided will leave us short of real freedom.

> So I sent to you immediately, and you have done well to come. Now therefore, we are all present before God, to hear *all the things* commanded you by God." (Acts 10:33).

Spiritual teenagers shouldn't wonder how life is going to work for them. Like David, they must know what God has already invested in us. Every journey that was taken by the Apostles was dedicated to everything that had already been accomplished (Acts 10:33 above). Their success did solely rest on the power that would transform the hearts of those who were ready to hear and accommodate all things. *All things* had supernatural boundaries, and the results as we read in the book of Acts were astounding.

> as His divine power has given to us *all things* that pertain to life and godliness…' (2 Peter 1:3)

If we only needed to know one or two things to overcome every manmade limitation, Jesus wouldn't have needed three years with His disciples. If Sunday sermons were enough, disciples wouldn't have needed to meet every day of the week. *"Day after day they met together…"* Acts 2:46. For spiritual teenagers to walk in God's divine ability, they will need an exposure to *all things*. This is going to take more than a glance into the Bible. It is going to take more than a multiple Sunday sermons. This will take some fellowship and communion with God.

> The Father loves the Son, and has given *all things* into His hand (John 3:35)

As spiritual teens, we would allow Jesus to be our Lord. Jesus is in all things and *all things* are in Jesus. We get access to *all things* when we believe in Him and our communion with Him releases all things. As spiritual teens, we aren't going to exercise anything independent of Jesus because we walk in the Spirit. The spirit of Christ provides the boundaries that we need. With *all things* within your reach, you aren't only going to discover yourself, you will change the forces that drive your life.

> When I was a child, I spoke as a child, I understood as a child, I thought as a child; but when I became a man, I put away childish things (1 Corinth. 13:11)

Regardless of the anointing and victories, spiritual teenagers aren't adults. Despite his victories as a youth, King David went on to face some moral challenges. Those who are merely spiritual teenagers can easily be challenged by their own flesh. As we purpose to grow into spiritual adults, we enter a place where "...*the body is dead because of sin; but the Spirit is life because of righteousness*" (Romans 8:10).

Note:

Even though the words '*all things*' were emphasized in this chapter, these words aren't particularly emphasized in the Holy Bible.

7

ADULT

- be Whole and Complete -

My encounter with a doctor who smokes is a very plain and clear example of the difference between our heads and our hearts. The doctor knows that it's stupid, yet it is an obvious heart issue. It is an example of why differences between our hearts and minds need to be resolved. There is a need for us to explore the boundaries which set our hearts and minds apart. As adults we know the limitations we have in our mind and flesh. Flesh is influenced by our five physical senses, that is by what we can see, taste, hear, smell and feel. However, your heart has eternity in mind.

> He has made everything beautiful in its time. Also He has put eternity in their hearts… (Ecclesiastes 3:11)

It was more than five years ago when doctors gave my sister six weeks to live. I was troubled like every other member of the family. It sounded as if she was given a death sentence. After spending some time in prayer, it occurred to me that the wording in the report we received had influenced our hearts incorrectly. My sister had not got six weeks to live. She has everlasting life (John 3:16). Her existence is eternal. Her spirit and soul will live forever. My sister's life had a very different foundation because, as I am going to show you, as spiritual adults, we are sustained by something more reliable than our head knowledge or our bodies. Doctors' conclusions were not based on my sister's spiritual life. They were based on the functionality of her body. So, let's look at the choice which helped my sister to battle her situation as an adult because we can all face the same challenges.

> Isn't there medicine in Gilead? Aren't there doctors there? Then why hasn't the health of my dear people been restored? (Jeremiah 8:22 God's Word Translation)

The above verse hints that our health is far beyond what medical doctors can restore. Meaning, our health can hang on to something that's more reliable than the prognosis from doctors' head knowledge. To most doctors, your life is tied to your body. They will most of the time talk of your body as if they are talking to the real you. To them, our existence is solely based on how our body functions. In other words, the end of your body is the end of your existence. Our bodies are treated as the ultimate thing that's keeping us alive. They will even be shocked if our attitude and beliefs don't seem to reflect that fact. While to doctors it is the body that's keeping you alive; to God, it's the heart [spirit + soul]. Your health isn't totally dependent upon your body.

> ...the body without the spirit is dead...
> (James 2:26)

We can thank God for our doctors. Jesus acknowledges the work of doctors (Matthew 9:12 and Luke 5:31). Above all, Colossians 4:14 reveals that the writer of one of the Gospels of Jesus, "Dr. Luke", was a physician. However, it's important to put our doctors in their place because, society seems to have made it so easy for us to quickly turn up on their doorstep in our times of crisis (i.e. 'local' GP in UK). The fact is, even though doctors are currently part of the picture because we live in the body, medical professionals shouldn't be the only place we turn to. According to the Bible, we're three-part beings. A mere care for our bodies isn't going to solve problems. When it comes to life, it is good to know how your spirit, your soul, and your body should all be taken into consideration.

> Now may the God of peace Himself sanctify you *completely*; and may your *whole* spirit, soul, and body be preserved blameless at the coming of our Lord Jesus Christ (1 Thessalonians 5:23)

I was not aware that all three parts of me 'spirit, soul and body' needed to function for my life to be complete. I would like you to pay attention to the words "complete" and "whole" in the above verse. Spiritual adults are whole and complete. We become whole and complete once all three parts of us are involved in the daily affairs of our lives. We don't want to merely let our bodies or souls determine the course of our life. Spiritual adults do not let their bodies determine or dictate who they are or what they do. In fact, even our great minds and personality, our "soul", wouldn't be big enough to save us. Ultimately, for us to be whole, we must not allow any of our three parts to be idle.

> For the flesh lusts against the Spirit, and the Spirit against the flesh; and these are contrary to one another, so that you do not do the things that you wish
> (Galatians 5:17)

Your born-again spirit isn't only immortal, it is as functional as other parts of your life. According to the Bible, your spirit is as functional as your body and soul *(...Paul was compelled by the Spirit... Acts 18:5, ...the fruit of the Spirit is love, joy, peace... Galatians 5:22-23)*. The lack of investment in your spirit will affect the equilibrium and dynamics which should exist between your three parts. Your spirit is also connected to forces that are far beyond your body and soul (...*the law of the Spirit of life*... Romans 8:2).

> For what man knows the things of a man except the spirit of the man which is in him? Even so no one knows the things of God except the Spirit of God (1 Corinthians 2:11)

While in the body we grow to die; in the spirit, we grow to live. ...*the inward man is being renewed day by day* (2 Corinthians 4:16). Your spirit is God's store-house because *God is Spirit*... (John 4:24). That's where God would place your spiritual treasures. ...*blessed us with every spiritual blessing*... (Ephesians 1:3). Hence, our adulthood depends on what's being fed into our spirit.

> It is the Spirit who gives life; the flesh profits nothing... (John 6:63)

I used to think my spirit had nothing to do with my daily life. I thought my spirit was something which stayed in there, dormant and bored, only to leave when I died. I thought that all I needed to excel in life was a functional working body, and an educated brain 'mind' in my soul. Actually, I thought that my spirit stayed in there waiting for me to get old, or become unfortunate enough to catch an incurable disease, or get drunk and drive over a bridge. It just stays in there and leaves once the doctors have failed to keep my body working. You see, such a mindset kept me an infant. I couldn't effectively deal with everything which might undermine my life. In the world, infant mortality rate is more likely to be higher than adult mortality rate. Those whose lives are fully invested in the body "children" can easily die. As it happens, my life was once crippled by ignorance of the investment which should have gone into my spirit.

> Now may the God of peace Himself sanctify you completely; and may your

> whole *spirit, soul, and body* be preserved
> blameless at the coming of our Lord
> Jesus Christ (1 Thessalonians 5:23)

As important as it is to be whole, according to the above verse, it is as important that our lives hinge on a very particular order. If we want God's cooperation, the Biblical order for our lives to be saved and served is spirit > soul > body. The Bible explains that whatever type of life is in your spirit will flow to your soul and then your body. In fact, this is the only order which can successfully maintain your health, wealth, and well-being. In my observation, whenever this order is reversed, lives have encountered huge problems. In other words, whatever else is allowed at the top of this order will eventually bring us down. For example, if my body comes first, doctors will be my first point of contact. Meaning, my doctor will have to be my deliverer/saviour or my prophet. However, unlike your doctors and philosophers who try to strengthen your body and mind, Jesus lives to strengthen your spirit and enables your body and soul as a result to receive supernatural victory.

> that He would grant you, according to the riches of His glory, to <u>be strengthened</u> with might through His Spirit in the inner man (Ephesians 3:16)

God knows that whatever comes first will be our defense and shield. If our bodies come first, they will be the one facing the enemy and determining what happens in our lives. That's why Jesus was quick to warn people, 'guys, even though I turned water into wine and multiplied food supernaturally, I didn't mainly come to serve/save your body (…*man shall not live by bread alone…* Mathew 4:4). I didn't primarily come to provide food for our bellies' or 'food for thought', but to provide eternal life in your spirit (…*the kingdom of God is not eating and drinking…* Romans 14:17, …*do not labor for the food which perishes…* John 6:26-27). Like the case of the doctor who found it impossible to stop smoking in his own strength, no amount of physical strength or intellectual influence can fully resolve my problems. That is why Jesus came to restore the correct life-giving order in our lives.

> Now a certain woman had a flow of blood for twelve years (Mark 5:25)

The woman with an issue of blood learnt it the hard way (Mark 5:25-34). I suspect that she didn't know that her body wasn't designed to confront the harsh realities of life on its own. She spent a lot of time and money with people who had already decided her fate. The medical professionals had already repeatedly failed her. After a chain of trial and errors, she realized that her doctors were not the ultimate help.

> …suffered many things from many physicians. She had spent all that she had and was no better, but rather grew worse (Mark 5:26).

It took a little bit of imagination for her to realize that her doctors' reports weren't the last report. When she heard about Jesus, she realized that she was suffering because she approached healing from a wrong standpoint. When she came across Jesus, she learned that there was nothing incurable. When she saw an opportunity to approach healing differently, she didn't hesitate to take a step. She was healed because she ended the cycle of approaching her healing from just a physical standpoint. *Immediately the fountain of her blood was dried up, and she felt in her body that she was healed of the affliction* (Mark 5:29). She became *whole and complete* when she saw her life in the spirit.

> For God is my witness, whom I serve with my spirit… (Romans 1:9)

Our only way of escape from the limitation of the body is to change the way we see life. Obviously, a reversed order 'body > soul > spirit' will get us to approach life as an infant. The order 'body >soul >spirit' brings your body into a place of prominence. When the order is reversed in this way, life feels a bit dyslexic and meaningless. That's why infants cry a lot. It is an approach which can leave us in a state of terror because it places greater value on the most vulnerable part of us – the body. Like children, those who dwell in the body needs a guardian. Our bodies aren't meant to lead us because they provide a very delicate boundary between life and death. They provide the enemy with an obvious victory because flesh is his territory. That's why Jesus maintained his life in the spirit. He rejected every attempt to bring his life down to his physical or biological connections (John 8:23).

> and raised us up together, and made us
> sit together in the heavenly places in
> Christ Jesus (Ephesians 2:6)

In the spirit, your boundaries are different. You are seated in the heavenly places (verse above). You aren't limited to the boundaries that your body has placed on your life. For example, the Jewish leaders once tried to trick Jesus by saying, *behold here are your brothers and sisters* (Matthew 12:47). They tried to keep Him within the boundaries that His earthly family had placed on Him. They were pointing to His biological siblings. Jesus responded by highlighting His spiritual family. *For whoever does the will of My Father in heaven is My brother and sister and mother."* (Matthew 12:50). He distanced Himself from every temptation to give His life in the flesh prominence over His spirit. His spiritual family/ relationships were more important than His biological/ physical relationships. It is an attitude that enabled Jesus to do the things no other person had done. I started to experience much greater freedom when I figured out the dynamics which should exist between my three treasure-stores 'spirit, soul and body'.

> I was in the Spirit on the Lord's Day, and I heard behind me a loud voice, as of a trumpet (Revelation 1:10)

The logic is quite simple. If the problem I faced lay in my body, then sports, food, and good sleep could have restored my wobbly frame to life. The people we look up to, or our cherished celebrities and worldly idols, could have been the healthiest, and most loving, and with the most enduring marriages/families. Obviously, they are already surrounded by world class food, people, and care. Aren't they? On top of that, if my problems such as anger and anxiety were merely triggered by my poor education, mind, intellect and emotions – that's 'soul' – I could have gotten out of every imaginable mess by exploiting philosophies, education and good friendships! My university degrees could have managed to keep me out of every trouble. However, I discovered that the answer to life's problems lay in the most forgotten part of our three part being – 'spirit'.

> For to be carnally minded is death, but
> to be spiritually minded is life and peace
> (Romans 8:6)

In fact, our transformation into adulthood starts when we acknowledge our body and soul's inability to deal with our key insecurities. That's when we also realize that we have ignored the most important part of our lives. If I were an aeroplane, my spirit is what's hidden behind the scene – within the fuselage. Life and conditions in the passenger space wouldn't be feasible without it. Before Christ changed my heart, that is where mood swings, fear, depression, and every health condition had their origin. Life and death, blessings and curses all have spiritual roots.

> For the law of the Spirit of life in Christ Jesus has made me free... (Romans 8:2)

A life that has only identified with the body will fail to benefit from the freedom we have as children of God. It is also more likely age faster because we wouldn't be able to stop worrying about what appears to be a definite end "death". When the body takes the prominent place in our lives, our perspective on our existence becomes time bound. That causes any signs of bodily ageing to breed fear, anxiety, and hopelessness. Even when lifestyle choices seem to have offered some delay tactics, we would subconsciously know that the clock is still ticking, even in the moment we thought it had stopped. However, when we get the very accurate picture of your new life in the spirit, we will not need to desperately turn back the clock because our lives are eternal.

> But if the Spirit of Him who raised Jesus from the dead dwells in you, He who raised Christ from the dead will also give life [heal] to your mortal bodies through His Spirit who dwells in you (Romans 8:11 – brackets mine)

Jesus started everything with the spirit. That helped him to see sickness and many of our difficulties differently. He called sickness the oppression of the devil (Acts 10:38). He saw that disabled limbs were twisted by the spirit of infirmity (Luke 13:11), and that the dumb were robbed of the power of speech by dumb spirits (Mark 9:25). To Him, the world had minds and bodies which were wrecked and tortured by cruel spirits (Mark 5:5; Luke 9:39). No amount of medical knowledge or science could fully resolve the problems Jesus confronted. To Him, what appears to be groundbreaking and serious scientific breakthrough can only ever deal with the bodily symptoms or side effects of our disconnection with God, and not the root cause. That is why Jesus commanded believers or those who have received life from the Spirit, to heal the sick (Mark 16:17-18). It's a commandment that gives all believers an opportunity to exercise their potential in the Spirit.

> And these signs will follow those who believe: In My name they will cast out demons; … they will lay hands on the sick, and they will recover
> (Mark 16:17-18)

Our survival is actually at risk from the moment we stop seeing ourselves in the spirit first. In other words, if my security is in my body, I will either have to give up or roll with the punches because life can, at times, become a little bit too strong to bear. My body will make my pain more real to me than the life which is on the inside of me. Wherever our bodies come first, we become vulnerable because whatever happens to our bodies will be decisive. Very simply, if what happens to our body determines our fate, our doctors can take that opportunity to decide when our time is up. As it turns out, the only way you can be faithful to your body, is by staying in the Spirit. Unlike our bodies, the Spirit never goes to sleep nor slumbers.

> He will not allow your foot to be moved; He who keeps you will not slumber… (Psalm 121:3-4)

Now, we can make a decision that matters. We can either walk in the freedom of the Spirit or embrace the body which will eventually hurt or disappoint us. The ageing family of Adam is biological and in bondage to sin. On the other hand, the eternal family of Christ is spiritual and free. We have an opportunity to decide where we're going to invest most of our time and energy.

If we choose the Spirit, we choose the life which isn't time-bound. Freedom reigns and time loses its grip on us when we join *the family* of Him who gives life to the spirit.

> **For** this reason I bow my knees to the Father of our Lord Jesus Christ, [15] from whom the *whole family in heaven and earth* is named (Ephesians 3:14-15)

8

FAMILY

- Join the Winning Team -

I remember watching the 2014 football World Cup semi-final match between Brazil and Germany with great anticipation. I couldn't help but wonder why so many people were shocked by the humiliation that Brazil faced in that semi-final match against Germany (Germany -7, Brazil -1). I hope you won't be put off at this point thinking this is all about football; NO! It's a 'faith' lesson to anyone who is intimidated by their personal world. The fact is, the results of that game carry truths which shouldn't only wow your view of sports. This could also transform the way you live your life, conduct your relationships and relate to your family. Once again, what appeared to have been an unpopular nonchalant German football team, utterly outplayed the potential winners! However, let's look into how the Brazilian team got such a beating, bearing in mind its huge talent.

Let's look at the German team as a family. Consider the path that's made the German team an all-time success. Their path holds some truths which will help you to identify and join the winning team. These truths are available to every one of us to exploit. As we'll see, Germany's success didn't rely on their playing as a clinical machine or their tactical innovation as some media guys have tried to suggest. It is important to remember that the once hopeful Argentina team had previously faced a similar upset (4-1) in a match against Germany in 2010. Their victories weren't a fluke as some would like to think either! They delivered what they received. They had a plan.

> For I received from the Lord that
> which I also delivered to you…
> (1 Corinthians 11:23)

To a trained eye, it would appear that the German football team has repeatedly delivered a game which is already tried, tested and proven. A player becomes part of the proven history and performance. Once we've adopted a life which is already tried, tested, and proven. Our experience is going to be very different. We would *be anxious for nothing* (Philippians 4:6). We would be *as bold as a lion* (Proverb 28:1). It is like coming into life knowing that victory is set before you. Despite their early exit in 2018, Germany have played semi-finals in 12 of the last 17 World Cup finals.

> Your ears shall hear a word behind you,
> saying, "<u>This is the way</u>, walk in it," …
> (Isaiah 30:21)

As it turns out, we all have the same opportunity. We have an opportunity to fit our life, family, business, dog, cat and whatever we can think of on a path that guarantees victory. In part, this has helped me to understand one of Jesus' popular phrases – '*the narrow path*'. A glimpse of the German team's path will be an answer to some misgivings you may have about the direction of your life. You will know all that you'll need to know to launch a victorious and fruitful life.

> Because strait is the gate, and *narrow* is
> the way, which leadeth unto life, and
> few there be that find it.
> (Matthew 7:14 KJV)

Well, we all love happy endings. But before that, let me point out one thing that will ever make the narrow path desirable to you – time (*Redeeming the time, because the days are evil...* Ephesians 5:16). The Brazilian team consistently failed to manage one of their most important assets – TIME. We all know that our life on earth isn't an endless journey. Like Jesus, we don't have forever to prove ourselves and make our life count. Every football player knows that they have 90 minutes to do what really matters – score goals. As we will see; once the last whistle is blown, everybody will forget all the wonderful tackles and ball possession we had. Unlike the Brazilian football team, you can take a path which will give you a lot of time to do what matters most. To Germany, 90 minutes provided no time for back-passes, seal-dribbles, and Cruyff-Turns. It's the results that matter (Germany-7, Brazil-1).

> All athletes are disciplined in their training. They do it to win a prize that will fade away, but we do it for an

eternal prize (1 Corinthians 9:25 New Living Translation)

Let's consider the narrow path as it applies to life, not football. When I say that the German team has consistently taken a "*narrow path*", some seem to get lost in those words. But the narrow path is simply a very well-defined path. It is defined in a way that leaves your opposition or enemy with very little room to maneuver. That's why during the actual game, the Brazilian team was busier, more stressed, and had to work harder than the German team. The narrow path is designed to fast-track your victory. That's why Germany seemed to get to the target a lot quicker than their opponents. With 225 goals, the German team is the highest scoring team in World Cup history. As it turns out, Jesus has shown us why what the world follows is still much inferior when compared to the narrow path he left to his believers.

> Let your eyes look straight ahead…
> (Proverbs 4:25)

Unfortunately for some people, the narrow path may seem to be as boring as the Germany game. It may seem to suggest that your life isn't necessarily going to grab all the headlines and the crowds aren't necessarily going to have much to cheer about. The path hasn't got room for little white lies or political correctness. We may not be able to keep up with our previous worldview of things. Like the Germany game, the absence of any fancy moves could seem to make your life less entertaining. Actually, it is my assumption that the German team knew that by sticking to their proven path, many onlookers would not enjoy their game. They'd be unpopular and wouldn't look as good on the television. No wonder most people in my part of the world were holding their breath for Brazil or Argentina to win the world cup. But, when all is said and done, results were the only thing that count; Germany –7, Brazil –1.

> Therefore by their fruits you will know them (Matthew 7:20)

There's so much to learn from the way Jesus accomplished what he had to accomplish with the short time he had on earth. Jesus used the story of *the Prodigal son* to show us how quickly the wide path can diminish our hope and steal from our future. Actually, it only took 30 minutes for the Brazilian crowds to be filled with tears, anguish, and brokenness. This wasn't long after their players had finished singing their national anthems with pride and confidence. Suddenly, their boisterous and vocal fans went quiet. Then, there were scenes of discouraged people leaving the stands by the droves. The Brazilian team was behind by 5-0 within 30 minutes. That's typical of a life in the wide path. It provides too many opportunities for us to wander through life aimlessly before falling into insignificance. The story of the Prodigal son reveals why we can afford very little time to wander away from the truth.

> Jesus said to him, "I am the way, the truth, and the life. No one comes to the Father except through Me (John 14:6)

The most encouraging thing is that life in the narrow path doesn't require gifts and talents to function. The German team didn't seem to have players who were popular, or as expensive or as naturally talented as the Brazilian team. Life in the narrow-path has only required of us to position ourselves correctly. This single fact has taken a lot of pressure off my life. It has taught me to keep my eyes off my talents. I could see why the German team has never required sophisticated or extremely gifted footballers. Furthermore, it is also a good clue as to why Jesus didn't seem to have considered gifts and talents when he was choosing his team of twelve disciples. He appears to have gone around and chosen those who were willing, without conducting any sort of detailed interviews. According to the Bible, the narrow path doesn't require those who are mighty, or wise, or noble.

> But God has chosen the foolish things of the world to put to shame the wise, and God has chosen the weak things of the world to put to shame the things which are mighty (1 Corinthians 1:27)

I hope you are beginning to see why the narrow path can provide us with an exceptional lifestyle. A lifestyle which doesn't require you to invent the way you're going to get your spouse, keep your mate, raise your children, accumulate wealth, or maintain your health. You are basically left with much less to deal with. You wouldn't need to rush around or be heavily dependent on drive-thru meals, instant coffees, and microwaved meals, because the narrow path leaves you with a lot of time to do what matters. Even when your life doesn't necessarily seem fancy on the surface, there's a guarantee that you'll be super effective. The German team knew that their game didn't engage the world, but was very dependable and somehow predictable.

> Do not turn to the right or the left…
> (Proverbs 4:27)

The fact is, once you've entered God's narrow path, your life will start to make sense. That is true for whatever situation you can think of. For example, if you want to be slim, the Bible's slimming-world is also in the narrow path because the wide-path is already filled with what shouldn't be eaten. Possibly, that's why the path is wide in the first place! It has room for unnecessary excesses. Jesus' narrow-path is created with your physical and mental health in mind. It has boundaries and borders which will keep you from falling into insignificance. Instead of being overwhelmed by options, you are kept in what the Bible calls – 'the perfect way of the Lord'.

> Now, therefore, you are no longer strangers and foreigners, but fellow citizens with the saints and members of the household of God (Ephesians 2:19)

Team is the key. The narrow-path is largely designed to reward 'teams'. You are a citizen of a kingdom. You are a member of a household. Real success would depend on the team, not some individuals. Like the heavenly Father, Son and Holy Spirit, the narrow path is designed to keep us closer and more sensitive to each other. The Brazilian football team somehow revealed the limitations of working as individuals. It appears that the failure of the Brazilian team came from their reliance on the input of only a few individuals. As it turns out, the absence of individuals like Neymar in the front line and Silva at the back, left the Brazilian world cup team with a defense that was able to be penetrated and a forward line that couldn't score goals. As you will see, a good team will take you to a place where you'll be able to enjoy the fruit of your commitment, integrity, and accountability.

> For as we have many members in
> one body, but all the members do
> not have the same function
> (Romans 12:4)

You may need to know a few things before you get involved in a team. First, you must have noticed that footballers do not create a team. They are just members. Second, they aren't in charge of the team either. Third, footballers are merely in charge of a position in a team. They are given a position with a well-designed purpose. Your success is purely dependent on you doing your part, faithfully fulfilling that purpose. As long as you do your part faithfully, you need not take responsibility for any losses. The only thing a good footballer needs to do is to identify a team and then join it. Likewise, we all have an opportunity to accept the invitation that God has given us to join His family, and not worry about the big picture.

> Behold, how good and how pleasant
> it is For brethren to dwell together
> in unity! (Psalm 133:1)

A team is a family. God has continually seen humanity in families. He has always had one family on the earth. It started with Adam, then Abraham [Jew] and later on Jesus [Christ]. The Bible is divided in a way that shows the transition from his covenant with the Jewish family into his covenant with the Christian family. Jesus Christ is God's greater effort to restore the lost world into his family. The Jewish family carried some promises which were going to be fulfilled in the Christian family. At the moment, every person breathing on earth today will either be in a Christian family or in the lost world.

> *The Jewish family* – the descendants of Jacob or the children of Israel (Exodus 4:22).
>
> *The Christian family* – a family that's open to whosoever will accept Jesus as Lord and Saviour (John 14:6).
>
> *The lost world* – this is the fallen and tragic world, searching for peace through its various religions and philosophies.

Life is a family business. No matter how smart we are, it isn't going to be possible for any one of us, as individuals, to cruise to our destiny. As we've already seen, professional players know that their vision, dreams, hopes, desires and victories are linked to their team's success. Any long-term success involves the team members. Every one of us has a part in the big picture. Professional players do not walk into a match with their own ideas. Instead of trying to invent our own life, let's move on to discover the life that's been offered to us by God through Jesus and then live it.

We need to be united in purpose because a victory of our own isn't sustainable. We were born to be adopted into this family. Our birth qualified us for a position which is already designed and established. If Jesus needed a company of 'disciples', we also probably need to be part of a team. As we have seen, the Prodigal Son tried to be a lone ranger (Luke 15:11-32). He thought that the world had room for solo acts. But, we have

God who has done all of what needs to be done for our joy to be fulfilled in His family.

> There is neither Jew nor Greek,
> …neither male nor female; for you are
> all one in Christ Jesus (Galatians 3:28)

There are a lot of Jews who are currently joining that family. They have discovered a better covenant and a better promise. This is something to celebrate because Jesus said that there's a homecoming party in heaven for everyone who's decided to join the family of God. Over centuries, this life-changing experience has had multiple other expressions such as salvation, becoming a believer, or coming into faith.

> Now you are the body of Christ, and
> individual members of it (1 Corinthians
> 12:27 KJV)

If we have been on our own, this is the time to change. Our lives shouldn't be limited to the family we were born into. God started his eternal family around 2000 years ago, also known as "the body of Christ". The body of Christ is our spiritual family. This is where children of God are born. We grow to become spiritual infants, toddlers and teenagers who are lavishing on His freedom. Unlike the way we were born into our biological families, the invitation into the body of Christ leaves us with a choice. This family gives you an opportunity to use the faith which Jesus had to enjoy the freedom he had. You are born free to live free.

Way forward…
- 🕐 Identify and join your family
- 🕐 Identify your position in the family
- 🕐 Execute your position faithfully
- 🕐 Share the victory

Prayers...

Prayer of
SALVATION

(You need to pray this prayer and believe in your heart as the words come out of your mouth)

Heavenly Father, I confess my need for a saviour (Romans 3:23). I come to You in the Name of Jesus for my Salvation (Acts 4:12). The Bible says, "Whosoever shall call on the name of the Lord shall be saved" (Acts 2:21). I repent of my sin (Romans 2:38, Acts 2:38). I am calling on You. I pray and ask Jesus to come into my heart and be Lord over my life (Acts 16:31). I'm responding to what you've said in the Bible *that if you confess with your mouth the Lord Jesus and believe in your heart that God has raised Him from the dead, you will be saved.* *¹⁰For with the heart one believes unto righteousness, and with the mouth confession is made unto salvation* (Romans 10:9-10).

I am now a brand-new person (2 Cor.5:17). I am born into the family of God (1 John 5:1). I am joined into the body of Christ (1 Cor. 12:27). I am a child of Almighty God (1 John 3:1)! I am eternally saved (Hebrews 5:9)! I am trusting you alone Lord Jesus. **Amen**!

Now, God would like you to be filled with His Holy Spirit (Acts 8:14-17, Acts 19:1-6) and be a disciple (Acts 11:26).

(Let us know if you would like more information on the Baptism in Water and Baptism in the Holy Spirit) Share your testimony WITH US.
passthenuggets@gmail.com

Prayer for

THE HOLY SPIRIT

(Please meditate the following verses as you ask and believe)

For everyone who asks receives, and he who seeks finds, and to him who knocks it will be opened. [11] If a son asks for bread from any father among you, will he give him a stone? Or if he asks for a fish, will he give him a serpent instead of a fish? [12] Or if he asks for an egg, will he offer him a scorpion? [13] If you then, being evil, know how to give good gifts to your children, how much more will your heavenly Father give the Holy Spirit to those who ask Him! (Luke 11:10-13)

'*And it shall come to pass in the last days, says God, That I will pour out of My Spirit on all flesh; Your sons and your daughters shall prophesy, Your young men shall see visions, Your old men shall dream dreams*' (Acts 2:17).

"*But you shall receive power when the Holy Spirit has come upon you…*" Acts 1:8

Father God, I ask in the name of Jesus, for the baptism of your Holy Spirit. I receive Him by faith right now. Thank you for baptizing me. **Amen**!

(Let us know if you want more information on Baptism in Water and Baptism in the Holy Spirit)

Let us know if you would like to share your testimony
passthenuggets@gmail.com

Prayer for
HEALING

(Note: we have prepared this prayer to supplement what you have already learned from this book) – pray this aloud.

Father God in the name of Jesus Christ I thank you for revelation of your desire to always heal (Peter 2:24, 3 John 1:2). I thank you because the sinless Son of God had to be stripped, bitten, whipped, chastised, smitten, and vehemently accused, mocked, scorned, ridiculed, crowned with thorns, bled, suffered, and die for me to receive healing in every area of my life (Isaiah 53:5). Thank you because your love and grace that can heal me even when my actions aren't good enough (Romans 5:8). I allow you right now to deal with what stands between me and the healing that you have provided to me on the cross (Acts 3:16). I command {name the specific situation i.e. asthma/peace} to be gone/restored/leave my body and life right now in the name of Jesus (Mark 11:23-24, Acts 4:10).

Thank you, God; thank you Jesus; thank you Holy Spirit. **Amen**!

(Take time to speak out your own personal words believing that God has already done it – 1John 5:14-15).

The Bible refers to a person 'Simon' who was 'poisoned by bitterness' (Acts 8:23). Please release yourself from any un-forgiveness you hold against anybody; or envy, or pride which the devil can use to keep you in bondage.

(Now, believe and stand on what you believe. Why? Because God is not a man, that He should lie (Num. 23:19)

– Share your testimony with us.

Thank you

Thank you for taking some time to read my book. Please REVIEW this book on <u>Amazon</u> to receive a free e-book of my next publication. While on Amazon, scroll down to find a tab with the title 'Write a customer review'. I need your feedback to make the next version better.

Share the love

Friends don't let friends miss a good thing. So, make them special. Offer them a copy as a Christmas or birthday present.

Other Bible references:

KJV – King James Version

GW – God's Word Translation (one verse) page 102

NLT – New living Translation (two verses) page 68, 125

Keep in touch:

🐦	twitter.com/rahaERNEST
f	facebook.com/faithNIBBLES
📷	instagram.com/rahaERNEST
📞	WhatsApp or Text +44 7950483516

Get The Audio Book Free!

Just to say thanks for writing a REVIEW on Amazon or sending us a testimony, I will also send you a download of the audio version of this book. Email to register your interest, 100% FREE!

(Available after 20th April 2020)

passthenuggets@gmail.com

ABOUT THE AUTHOR

Raha Ernest is married to Susan with whom they are blessed to have four children. From the moment Raha received Jesus as Lord and Saviour on 20th January 2002, God birthed within him a vision to share the Good News of the supernatural transformation that comes with accepting Jesus as Saviour. Raha is a graduate of Charis Bible College, University of Nottingham and AA School of Architecture in England, and Ardhi University in Tanzania.

www.faithNibbles.com
twitter.com/rahaERNEST
instagram.com/rahaERNEST
facebook.com/faithNIBBLES

Printed in Poland
by Amazon Fulfillment
Poland Sp. z o.o., Wrocław